FROM TRASH TO TREASURE

How Holding on to the Trash of Life Can Hinder Your Treasure in Life

TOSHA SMITH

Dear Reader,

As you embark on this transformative journey, remember that within you lies the power to turn your life around, to shed the weight of past burdens, and to embrace the limitless possibilities that await you.

The path to a new level of joy, peace, and fulfillment begins with a willingness to let go of what no longer serves you and to open your heart to new beginnings.

Get ready to dive deep into my raw and transparent life journey in the first installment of 'From Trash To Treasure.' Stay tuned for more captivating chapters as I share my story through my unique lens, unveiling the highs and lows, the triumphs and tribulations.

Join me on this transformative adventure as we uncover the treasures hidden within the depths of my experiences. The journey has just begun, and there's so much more to explore!

With love and encouragement,

- Tosha Smith

What is Trash & What is Treasure?

DEFINING AND UNDERSTANDING THE TWO

An analogy between the trash in our lives and the clutter in a landfill, making it harder for us to appreciate the treasures life has to offer. Let's dive deeper into the idea that handling both the trash and the treasures in our lives requires care to avoid hindering our path to happiness and peace.

Definition of **Trash**- a person or people regarded as being of very low social standing.

Definition of **Treasure**- Things that people value above all else and that motivate them to take action.

Identifying the Trash: Just like in a landfill, it's essential to identify the sources of trash in our lives. These could be negative thoughts, toxic relationships, harmful habits, or unproductive patterns. Recognizing and acknowledging these aspects is the first step towards decluttering our lives.

Handling the Trash: Once we identify the trash, we must handle it carefully. This involves actively working to eliminate or manage the negative influences that weigh us down. It could mean letting go of toxic relationships, seeking help for harmful habits, or changing our perspective on negative situations.

Protecting the Treasures: On the flip side, treasures in our lives represent the positive aspects that bring us joy, fulfillment, and peace. These could be meaningful relationships, personal achievements, cherished memories, or moments of gratitude. It's crucial to protect and nurture these treasures amidst the chaos of daily life.

Balancing Act: Balancing the management of trash and treasures is key to our overall well-being. Sometimes, we may need to make tough decisions to prioritize our mental and emotional health over certain relationships or commitments that no longer serve us. This delicate balance requires self-awareness, introspection, and the courage to make necessary changes.

Clearing the Path to Happiness and Peace:
By effectively managing the trash and safeguarding the treasures in our lives, we clear the path to finding happiness and peace. Decluttering our physical space, practicing mindfulness, fostering positive relationships, and pursuing activities that bring us joy are all ways to create a more fulfilling and harmonious life.

This book tells part of my story and journey but ultimately highlights the importance of being mindful of what we allow into our lives, taking proactive steps to remove negativity, and nurturing the positive aspects that enrich our existence. By carefully handling the trash and treasures in our lives, we pave the way for a more meaningful, joyful, and peaceful journey. Just as the image you see here Our lives can become cluttered with emotional trauma, depression, violence, toxic relationships, and so much more, but you must find yourself doing the exact thing we see in the picture, removing and discarding what hurts or hinders us in life that cause us so much pain, darkness, fear, ect all forms of trash.

DEDICATION

This book is dedicated to every reader whose life has been destroyed, challenged, and felt to have no value. I dedicate this to you because no matter how many of life's most difficult tests and trials you endured, you made it! You beat the odds, disposed of the trash in your life, stood the test; fought the good fight, kept the faith, and found the treasures in your life. So here's to you! May every word you read bless you tremendously.

To my husband, Michael, you are such an amazing husband. The day I met you I found my missing piece. You complete me and make me a better person. I'm so grateful to be doing life with you, you are everything I need when I need it. I love and honor you, my King of the earth, and appreciate you for accepting me, flaws and all. Life now is worth living because you are there to ensure I know what love, loyalty, and support looks like. You push me, motivate me, and encourage me to shoot for the stars in all that I do. I'm so blessed to have you in my world, you're my friend that I never have to question, you love me the way I need to be loved, and for that, I'm grateful.

To my mother, Carolyn. You, who had set aside your own pen to pave the way for my journey, I carry with me the legacy of your unwritten words. It is in your sacrifice that I found purpose. With every stroke of the pen, I write not only for myself but for you, carrying forward the torch you once held so dearly. Thank you for giving me not just life, but also inspiration .This book is not just mine, but ours.

To my children(Shawn, Quindarius, Saniya, Am'Ariah, Michaela, Anastasia), My team, and my tribe! There would be a different life for me without you all in it. (My true treasures) We've gone through many trials together. You all have observed many things that I've done in life, both good and bad. I thank God that I got it right before it was too late. I want you all to know that you too, can dispose of it all, you do not have to harbor it, it can be disposed of. Finding the treasure of your life will help each of you tremendously. We have always been each other's strength. I'm so blessed to carry the title of Mom to such extraordinary individuals. Thank you for trusting me to lead you all. You all are the reason change was necessary; Mommy loves you.

In Loving Memory of My Father

Herman "DJ Boogieman" Dyson

I dedicate this book to the memory of my father, Herman "DJ Boogieman" Dyson, whose presence in my life continues to inspire and guide me. Though his physical presence may be absent, his spirit lives on in the pages of this work.

I thank him for the gift of life, for the lessons learned, and for the love he shared. Through forgiveness, I have found peace and the strength to transform pain into purpose. It is through his absence that this book was able to be birthed, a testament to the power of healing and growth.

May his memory be a blessing, and may his legacy live on through the words written here.

With love and gratitude,

💜 Your Daughter, Tosha 💜

Daddy's Girls

Daddy I'm still here

Daddy's Gang

ACKNOWLEDGEMENTS

I would like to express my deepest gratitude to all those who have contributed to the creation of this book, "From Trash to Treasure." Without your support, encouragement, and inspiration, this project would not have been possible.

I am immensely thankful to my family for their unwavering love, understanding, and patience throughout this journey. Your support has been my strength.

To my friends and colleagues who have provided valuable feedback, insightful discussions, and endless encouragement, I am truly grateful for your contributions.

A special thank you to the experts and professionals in the field of Publishing and

Formatting who generously shared their knowledge and expertise, enriching the content of this book.

I extend my appreciation to my editor and writing Coach, Tyneshia Reed, for your meticulous attention to detail, constructive feedback, and dedication to refining this manuscript.

I am indebted to Arif Hossain for his guidance, professionalism, and commitment to bringing this book to life.

Lastly, to the readers who will embark on this journey of transformation with me, thank you for your interest and support. It is my hope that "From Trash to Treasure" inspires you to see beauty and potential in unexpected places.

Thank you all for being a part of this remarkable experience.

With heartfelt thanks,

- Tosha Smith

PREFACE

Welcome to "From Trash to Treasure"!

Within these pages, you will embark on a journey of transformation, resilience, and hope. This book is a testament to the remarkable power that lies within each of us to turn our setbacks into stepping stones and our pain into purpose.

Life is filled with moments that may leave us feeling broken, discarded, or lost. But remember, just like a diamond in the rough, our true beauty and strength often emerge from trials and tribulations we face. This book is a celebration of the human spirit and the incredible capacity we have to rise above adversity and turn our lives from mere existence to extraordinary existence.

As you delve into my story of how I was able to turn my "Trash" into "Treasure," may you find inspiration, courage, and a renewed sense of purpose. Remember, no matter how difficult your circumstances may seem, there is always a path forward, a way to transform your challenges into opportunities and your pain into power.

I invite you to open your heart and mind as you journey through these pages. Let the stories within serve as a beacon of hope, a reminder that no matter how dark the night may seem, the dawn always breaks, bringing with it new beginnings and endless possibilities.

Thank you for joining me on this transformative journey. May you discover the treasure that lies within you and find the strength to turn your own challenges into triumphs.

With hope and gratitude,

-Tosha Smith

TABLE OF CONTENTS

INTRODUCTION
FROM TRASH TO TREASURE

How Holding On To The Trash of Life Can Hinder Your Treasure in Life

In the tapestry of our existence, we often find ourselves entangled in the remnants of the past, clinging onto the debris that life has thrown our way. These remnants, these pieces of trash, may come in many forms- Be it regrets, mistakes, heartbreaks, or even missed opportunities. They weigh us down, cloud our vision, and hinder our ability to see the true treasure that lies ahead.

What if, instead of carrying this weight, we choose to confront it head-on? What if we choose to forgive, not for the sake of those who wronged us, but for our own liberation? What if we activated the transformative power of letting go - of shedding the layers of hurt and resentment, of freeing ourselves from the shackles of anger and pain?

In my reflection on my personal journey, I reveal how the obstacles and challenges in my life served as barriers that obstructed my path to discovering the treasure within. Through my experiences, I offer insights and guidance to inspire you to let go of the burdens and negativity holding you back, and to embark on your own transformative journey towards uncovering your hidden treasures.

CHAPTER- 1
THE WEIGHT OF BETRAYAL AND HURT

Carrying the burdens of our past -be it hurt, betrayals, obstacles, divorce, unforgiveness, or other emotional burdens is like dragging a heavy bag of trash wherever you go in life. This baggage weighs you down, sapping your energy, clouding your judgment and, preventing you from moving forward freely. The longer you hold on to this emotional trash, the harder it becomes to see the treasures waiting for you on the horizon.

It's essential to recognize that the weight of this baggage not only affects you but also impacts your relationships, career, and overall well-being. The longer you carry it, the more it seeps into every aspect of your life, hindering your ability to grow and thrive.

In the darkness of despair, when betrayal

cuts deep and the whispers of gossip echo in the corridors of our minds, it is easy to get lost in the shadows of our past. The wounds inflicted by those we trusted, the scars left by those who treated us as less than we are, can become the heavy burdens we carry with us, day in and day out. We hold on to the trash of our past, the hurt, and the pain, allowing it to shape our present and dictate our future.

As I sat there one Wednesday afternoon, My mind began to go back through my journey. I asked myself when did the trash start to form in my life? What caused this landfill of debris to overtake me and cause so many bad choices, wrong decisions, hurt, pain and betrayal? Why am I lost in the sea of my own pain? What can I do to escape these emotions and find a space where I'm glowing, happy, at peace with who I am? I had to start from the moment in my life where I felt a shift in the person I was destined to be. So I began to cry because instantly I was taken back to around the age of 12 years old. My childhood was shattered due to molestation and abuse, **(Betrayal)**, this is a form of trash, which broke me and made me numb to everything. I lost my joy at an early age, I became sad and timid. I went from this happy energetic little girl to being closed off and always feeling like I had to hide. The more twisted part was that I still had to be around the person who took advantage of my youth.

I couldn't go to anyone, so I had to endure that hurt and shame for years. I didn't have the courage to tell. I was very much afraid. So as I sat there and thought, I knew that the only way for me to get to the point where my life could change I had to go back, forgive the people that hurt me and caused me this level of trash pile up, more importantly I had to start the forgiving process with me.

Now as I continue to sit there I began to ask God to take me back and heal every place that caused me to hold on to this trash in my life, at that very moment I went back in time on a journey of my life. I then envisioned myself in middle school being different from the other children and caused me to be bullied a lot. They would make fun of my clothing, my hair, call me Olive Oyl because I was so skinny and that was a sad time for me. **(Low self-esteem) a form of trash**.

I silently cried a lot in my preteen years. Mentally, at that young of an age I barely made it. I would often hear a voice say "kill yourself" (**Sucide**) **a form of trash.** Now as I lay there the tears are uncontrollable, because I'm looking into my childhood with a different set of eyes, now thankful that I made it and I can talk about overcoming. I'm now in the memory of my High School years, my life became worse because I carried darkness around like a purse.

I became ashamed and angry. (**Offense**) **a form of trash.** I questioned myself daily, I couldn't understand why things happened to me as they were happening. It was like my mind was so confused. Sometimes I would listen to that voice and try to take my own life, because it seemed as if life was not for me

I was mocked constantly for being different, and skinny, the name calling went from Olive Oyl to them calling me bones. I would agree with my peers about my looks. (**Lack of self- confidence**) another form of trash, definitely not popular and less fortunate than most of my peers.

Being spit on, hit on, and degraded caused me pain for many years. Then the children from school made my life even worse. All the while I was constantly in fear of my accuser because he was always around. It's as if he would be around to make sure I never said anything.

I struggled for years! But as I got older I tried telling myself that's a part of my life that I've gotten over, but the reality was I didnt get over it. I just took it to the landfill of hidden trash that would surface later. The older I became the more I based how I was treated as a right to form the attitude that "I would do people just how people do me" **(Vengeance)** another form of trash. I would get into relationships that were so toxic and abusive and were often taken advantage of, but that was a normal relationship so I thought.

So unaware, Choosing partners based on how I was treated; showing love was definitely out the window! I found myself in relationships with no thoughts or expectations of love and loyalty because, hey it was never given to me! **(An eye for an eye)** another form of trash. I trusted no one; telling me that you loved me was like telling me the sky was red. 'I knew it wasn't true.' I became a person I never imagined I'd become. How did such an amazing and sweet girl end up here? I turned cold. Bitterness, hurt, and betrayal, took control of my life. **(Detached)** another form of trash.

While the trash of life made itself at home, The weight of it caused me to make choices and decisions that I would regret later in life.

Because of the hurt and anger from incidents in my life I became tangled in things I never thought I would do. In the mid 90's, my trash of life brought me to an even darker place. That's when I started to escort women. Yes, I made a business out of it. I moved hours away so no one who knew me knew what I had become. I gained the trust of women only to reverse the same pain onto them that was done to me; I would often say to myself that I was nothing like my accuser or even like pimps for that matter, because when I made connections for men to be with these women, when I profit, they did too.

I got so comfortable in that life! I was known as Madam T. I thought it was cool then, I was liked for the first time in life from people who were not my immediate family.

I was misguided, hurt, and vengeful. I was living a fast and dangerous life. All the while I was causing trash build-up in others' lives. Not realizing the power I had in shaping the emotional landscape of those I encountered.

Just as a discarded item can become an eyesore or a burden to others, my actions and deeds created emotional debris such as embarrassment, hurt, and insecurities in the lives of these women. I transformed what was once a momentary misstep into a heavy load of emotional waste for them to bear. I had no clear vision of my actions.

I caused so much pain, unaware, all because of the pain I was carrying from my past. It took me years, and an arrest for me to leave that lifestyle, but just like many forms of trash in life, although I removed myself from it, I didn't dispose of the trash from that lifestyle properly. Which caused me to jump from one negative thing to another negative thing,

It's now 1999. I'm in the prime of my life. I'm young and still not fully realizing how my actions are causing the trash to pile. Influenced by an ex, I sold drugs for

10

the majority of my young adult life. (You see, harboring trash will always attract more trash.) I did anything to make my mind, not program the past trauma. I was involved in so many illegal things. It was a constant looking over my shoulders.

From drug use, to selling and delivering, addicted to pills and alcohol. I would frequently just do it to not think about my past or present life. It got so bad that I would often think about ending my life. It just doesn't seem so bad I'd often say. I remember at one point I sat down and wrote a letter to my mom apologizing and asking her to take care of my son and tell him I was sorry I wasn't strong enough to stay and raise him. That was a very dark time in my life. You'll hear more about that in the many series to come.

I recount the experience of coming face to face with the darkest thoughts that almost led me to take my own life. All this trash had been accumulating in my life, the bad relationships, unfulfilled dreams, relentless struggles, and overwhelming sense of hopelessness. Each piece of trash represented a painful memory, a shattered dream, or a deep-rooted fear of something. The weight of the trash had gotten the best of me. I found myself standing on the edge of despair.

The voices of **self-doubt** and **self-condemnation** (forms of trash) echoed loudly in my mind, drowning out any sign of hope or light. Most of the battles I faced were within. Fighting the battle between whether to hold on or let go, between choosing life or accepting death. I share the raw emotions, the tears shed in secret, and the silent screams that ripped through my soul as I fought with the idea of ending it all.

Even in my darkest moments, there was always a still small voice that pierced through the shadows, a moment of clarity, that whisper of hope that reminded me of the love and support that surrounded me, even in my darkest hour. It was at that moment that I realized that my life was worth fighting for.

That I was more than the sum of my struggles. But even in the heat of it all, I still chose a life that I knew wasn't for me to partake in. See when you're in so deep you'll find yourself drowning in darkness and wrong doings. Mostly without even being aware you'll become deeper in your own darkness, this is where I was when my life was in the hands of the enemy. So caught up that I couldn't see what was coming ahead.

CHAPTER- 2
THE CLOSE CALL

I was caught up in that lifestyle of drug dealing, prostitution, the fast money, the feeling of power, and the sense of invincibility that I didn't see the future of what could happen to me. This very lifestyle almost led me to my death for the second time. All the risks and dangers I chose to ignore in pursuit of profit meet me at the barrel of a 9- millimeter, demanding that I give up all I had or die.

That cold metal of the gun pressed against my temple sent a shockwave of fear through my body. Time seemed to slow down as I stared into the eyes of the person holding the gun, their finger tightening on the trigger. In that heart-stopping moment, I realized the gravity of the choices I had made and the dangerous path I had been walking.

It all started innocently enough, a quick way to make some extra cash and to prove I was loyal. But the allure of easy money and acceptance soon led me down a dark and treacherous road. I became entangled in the web of drug dealing, blinded by the false promises of love, wealth and power. I thought because of my gender, I was invincible, untouchable. But that illusion shattered in an instant as the guy stood before me, ready to end my life.

They made me undress, I was so afraid of being raped and killed. In that moment, feelings of fear took over, but so did regret and disbelief. All I could do was beg for my life, then, all of a sudden I could see a vehicle coming from afar.

I knew my life was about to be spared, I just knew. In the heat of the moment there was this feeling of hope. The other guy yelled, "she saw our face man." He looked at me and pulled the trigger with the gun upward. As the sound of the gunshot echoed in the air, I felt a rush of adrenaline and a surge of gratitude for another chance at life.

The other guy screamed again, "shoot

her." Oh the look in his eyes changed, and I knew I was dead. He pulled the trigger, and the gun would not go off. (talk about your angels being with you) The bullet missed its mark by grace and mercy. Sparing me from a fate I could never have imagined. That vehicle that was approaching pulled over on the side of the highway, a ways up from where all was taking place. A tall, slender man arose from the vehicle and yelled "Ma'am, are you ok"? He screams hey leave her alone, I've called the cops!

I looked over and screamed "help me please". They both grabbed the money and the bag and ran to their vehicle. As they sped off, I began to run towards the man standing in the door of his vehicle. He opened his back door, pulled out a long khaki coat and said here, ma'am cover up, you're safe now, help is on the way. In that moment of reckoning, I knew I had to make a change.

I had to turn my life around before it was too late. In sharing this deeply personal chapter of my life, I hope to inspire others who may be facing their own battles with despair and hopelessness. I want you to know that even in the darkest of times, there is always a glimmer of light, a thread of hope that can lead you out of the shadows and into a brighter tomorrow. May my story serve as a beacon of courage, resilience, and redemption for you all who are struggling to find your way From Trash to Treasure.

CHAPTER- 3
THE AWAKENING

The brush of death was a wake-up call that reverberated through my being, shaking me to my core. As I replayed the events of that fateful day in my mind, I saw with clarity the wreckage of my past choices and the destruction they had wrought. The near-death encounter had opened my eyes to the harsh reality of my situation, forcing me to confront the darkness that had consumed me.

In the days that followed, I struggled with a mix of emotions- fear, regret, relief, and yet a glimmer of hope. I knew that I couldn't continue down the path of self-destruction any longer. It was time to break free from the chains, to shed the cloak of "trash" that had defined me for so long and unearth the hidden treasure buried within. I knew it would be a challenge. I've been in this lifestyle too long. Although this incident caused me to step back, look at life and change the reality, I was in too deep and knew it would be a ton of hindrances that would try and stop me.

As I laid there thinking, I couldn't help but to feel the weight of my past choices pressing down on me like a heavy burden. The allure of my dangerous lifestyle, with its thrills and escapades, still lingered in the back of my mind, tempting me to return to the familiar comfort of recklessness. The fear of the unknown and the uncertainty of change loomed large, casting a shadow over my newfound resolve to turn my life around.

Despite my sincere desire to heal and let go of the destructive patterns that had brought me to the brink of disaster, I knew that the road to redemption would not be easy. The deeply ingrained habits and behaviors that had defined me for so long now stood as formidable obstacles on my path to transformation.

The friends that had egged me on in my wild pursuits now whispered doubts and skepticism, sowing seeds of doubt in my mind (also a form of trash) and testing my commitment to change. My scars of past traumas and unresolved emotional wounds served as constant reminders of the pain and turmoil that had driven me toward my dangerous lifestyle in the first place. The fear of facing my inner demons and confronting the demons of my past threatened to derail my journey toward healing and self-discovery.

It became clear to me that true transformation would require not only courage and determination but also a willingness to delve into the depths of my soul, unearth the buried truths, and confront the shadows that lurked within. Only by acknowledging and overcoming these hindrances could I hope to truly let go of my dangerous past and embrace a brighter, more fulfilling future.

CHAPTER- 4
HINDRANCE TO HEALING

Holding on to the trash of life acts as a barrier to healing and growth. It keeps you stuck in a cycle of pain and resentment, preventing you from fully embracing new opportunities and experiences. Just as a wound cannot heal if it is constantly exposed to dirt and infection, your emotional wounds cannot heal if they are continuously reopened by holding on to past hurts and unforgiveness.

This emotional baggage can also impact your physical health, leading to stress, anxiety, and other negative consequences. It's like carrying a heavy burden on your shoulders, causing strain and exhaustion that permeates every aspect of your life. By not allowing myself to truly heal, it caused me so much hurt, hindered my levels of trust for genuine people, and caused me to not want friends and people who were actually good for my life. It definitely made me not trust any relationship.

The trash was piling, and I thought that because I handled it so well, I was healed from it all. I had to truly learn to sift through the trash of my past and uncover the hidden treasures that lie beneath. It is only by facing our shadows, and embracing our pain, that we can truly move forward and unlock the treasures that await us on the other side of forgiveness.

"Clutching onto hurtful memories and emotions acts as a heavy anchor, dragging down the sails of progress in the voyage of self-healing. For years, I clung tightly to the shards of painful experiences, allowing them to puncture my heart repeatedly.

The very act of holding onto these hurtful things postponed my healing journey, trapping me in a cycle of bitterness and resentment. Each memory acted as a chain, binding me to the past and preventing me from embracing the present moment fully."

"As I sifted through the wreckage of my past, I realized that my unwillingness to let go of these hurtful things was akin to choosing to carry a burden that was never mine to bear. The weight of resentment and anger kept me shackled to a version of myself that no longer existed, hindering any chance of genuine healing and growth. Only when I mustered the courage to release these toxic emotions did I begin to feel the gentle breeze of healing caress my soul, slowly but surely guiding me towards a brighter, more liberated future."

CHAPTER- 5
BREAKING FREE

To break free from the hindrance of emotional baggage, you must first acknowledge its existence and the toll it is taking on your well-being. Recognize that holding on to the trash of life is a choice and that you have the power to let go. Practice self-compassion and forgiveness towards yourself and others, understanding that carrying this baggage is not serving your highest good.

By letting go of the past, you create a space for new beginnings and positive transformations in your life. Seek out healthy coping mechanisms such as mindfulness, journaling, therapy, or support groups to help you process your emotions and release the weight of emotional baggage that has been holding you back. Remember that healing is a journey, and it's okay to seek help and support along the way.

By this time in my life I had already gone through some of life's most difficult moments, married (scared into the marriage by the saints) with two sons already. I'm now 29 years old and pregnant again, back into selling drugs and many other illegal things, but this pregnancy is different, it's my first daughter, and all I could think about was my life as a young girl and how to prevent things from happening to my daughter. My sons, I automatically knew they would not have to go through and endure certain things in life as a girl would. I knew I had to do something different. Having my daughter was a powerful catalyst for my healing and personal growth.

The deep love and bond between parent and child can inspire profound transformation. The desire to protect and nurture her, to shield her from the pain and struggles I endured, motivated me to confront and release the emotional baggage that weighed me down. Through my role as her mom I was given the opportunity to break the cycle of generational trauma and provide a safe and nurturing environment to thrive and flourish, for not just my daughter, but my other two children also.

My love for my children became a driving force that propelled me to self-discovery, self-compassion, and forgiveness. The beginning of my journey to finding my treasure. I had to realize that by healing from the trash in my life, I not only created a brighter future for myself but also laid the foundation for a legacy of resilience, strength, and love that I was able to pass on to my sons and my daughter ensuring that they grow up in an environment filled with love, understanding, and support.

CHAPTER- 6
CULTIVATING RESILIENCE

Building resilience is essential in overcoming the challenges posed by holding on to emotional baggage. I was so in a state of emotional damage that it caused me to be offended often. (that's another form of trash). I was always on guard about everything. When there were times I had no reason to feel that way about anything, yet I was. This caused me to have mental mind battles daily. Unstable in all my ways.

I stayed in that state of mind for a long time before I was able to cultivate a mindset of growth and resilience. Cultivating resilience from the trash in your life can have a profound impact on how you navigate and appreciate the treasures you have found. Resilience allows you to face challenges with a sense of inner strength and determination, enabling you to bounce back from setbacks and adversities.

By developing resilience, you are better equipped to handle life's ups and downs without being overwhelmed by negative emotions or setbacks. This newfound strength enables you to approach life's challenges with a positive mindset and a belief in your ability to overcome obstacles.

Moreover, cultivating resilience from past hurts and struggles empowers you to live more authentically and purposefully. It helps you shed the weight of emotional baggage that has held you back, allowing you to embrace your true self and live in alignment with your values and aspirations. Resilience gives you the courage to step out of your comfort zone, take risks, and pursue your dreams with unwavering determination. As you let go of the past and focus on building your resilience you free yourself from constraints of self-doubt and fear, opening up a world of possibilities and opportunities.

Furthermore, resilience enhances your relationships and connections with others, fostering deeper bonds and a sense of community. As you cultivate resilience, you become a source of strength and support for those around you, inspiring others to face their own challenges with courage and determination. Your ability to overcome adversity and bounce back from setbacks serves as a beacon of hope and encouragement for others who may be struggling. I am the definition of overcoming what tried to overtake me.

RESILIENCE

The strongest oak of the forest is not the one that is protected from the storm and hidden from the sun. It's the one that stands in the open where it is compelled to struggle for its existence against the winds and rains and the scorching sun.

Napoleon Hill

CHAPTER- 7

EMBRACING TRANSFORMATION

"In the journey **From Trash to Treasure**, betrayal often emerges as a formidable adversary that stealthily creeps into our lives, leaving behind a trail of heartache and mistrust. Betrayal, with its sharp claws of deceit, has the insidious ability to linger long after the initial wound has been inflicted. Like a shadow that refuses to be shaken off, it follows us, tainting our perceptions and hindering our ability to forge ahead toward our destined treasure.

The weight of betrayal can be crushing, burdening our spirits, and impeding our progress as we navigate the winding paths of life. Yet, it is in confronting this trash, in acknowledging its presence and its impact, that we pave the way for healing and transformation. Only by facing the darkness of betrayal can we truly illuminate the path to our ultimate treasure." After life threw me so many hard balls, I had to come to the realization that a change was necessary and it must start with me first.

I had to work through the process of releasing the trash of life, I created a space for transformation, growth, and new experiences. My mind had to now focus more on gratitude, possibilities, and positivity, as well as celebrating the small victories along the way. By letting go of past hurts, betrayals, obstacles, divorce, vengeance, unforgiveness, and all other things one may harbor in the landfills, filled with emotional trash, you pave the way for a brighter future for yourself to be vulnerable and open.

The only way to reach the treasures in life I had to work through my landfield of trash and release it. It is possible to create a space for transformation and growth. Instead of focusing on everything that's going wrong, embrace the journey of self-discovery and healing, allowing your heart, mind, spirit, and soul to forgive.

CHAPTER- 8

REDEMPTION AND RENEWAL

In the depths of my despair, surrounded by the wreckage of my past mistakes and poor choices, I found myself at a crossroads. The weight of hurt and betrayal threatened to consume me, while the shackles of unforgiveness bound me to a life of darkness. I was lost in a cycle of self-destructive behavior, seeking solace in the temporary escape that drugs provided. It seemed like my life was destined to be nothing more than a cautionary tale, a cautionary tale of how easily one could fall from grace.

Yet, in the midst of this chaos and despair, a glimmer of hope began to flicker within me. It was a small, fragile spark at first, barely noticeable amidst the wreckage of my past. But as I reflected on the path that had led me to this point, I began to see that the very things that had once held me back could be the keys to unlocking a brighter future. The pain and suffering I had endured had not broken me; they had tempered me, shaping me into a stronger, more resilient version of myself.

As I delved deeper into my past, confronting the demons that had long haunted me, I began to see a path forward. Through the power of forgiveness, both for others and for myself, I discovered a newfound sense of freedom and peace. The drugs that had once offered me false comfort now held no sway over me; I had found a deeper, more lasting source of solace within myself. From the ashes of my former life, I began to build something new, something beautiful—a life transformed from trash to treasure.

CHAPTER- 9
EMBRACING LIBERATION

THE TRANSFORMATIVE POWER OF FORGIVENESS

From the depths of betrayal towards the promise of treasure, one powerful antidote emerges from the shadows: Forgiveness. Forgiveness is not about excusing the actions of others or forgetting the pain they may have caused us. Instead, it is a conscious choice to release the hold that past hurts have over our present and future. By forgiving those who have wronged us, we free ourselves from the cycle of bitterness and resentment that can poison our hearts and minds.

In letting go of anger and hurt, we create space for healing and growth, paving the way for new opportunities and treasures to

34

enter our lives. True forgiveness is a gift we give ourselves, a key that unlocks the door to our own inner peace and happiness. It is a courageous act of self-love and empowerment that allows us to reclaim our power and chart a course towards the treasures that await us.

By embracing forgiveness, we can transform our trash-filled past into a treasure trove of lessons learned, wisdom gained, and a renewed sense of purpose and possibility for the future. In the depths of despair and surrounded by what seemed like an endless sea of darkness, I found myself standing at the crossroads of hopelessness and faith. It was in those moments of utter desperation that I turned to God, seeking solace and guidance amidst the chaos that had consumed my life.

As I opened my heart to the possibility of divine intervention, a flicker of light pierced through the shadows, illuminating a path that led me from the depths of despair to the promise of redemption.

With each step I took on this newfound journey of faith, I felt the weight of my burdens slowly lifting, replaced by a sense of peace and clarity that I had never known before. The once overwhelming darkness that had clouded my vision began to dissipate, revealing a world brimming with possibility and hope. It was as if God had reached down from the heavens, gathering up the shattered pieces of my life and gently guiding me towards a path of healing and transformation.

As I delved deeper into my newfound faith, I began to see the beauty in the brokenness that had once defined my existence. What I once saw as trash and wreckage now revealed itself to be the raw materials from which God was crafting a masterpiece. Each trial and tribulation, every moment of despair and doubt, served as a brushstroke in the divine tapestry of my life, weaving together a story of redemption and grace that surpassed all understanding.

Through the lens of faith, I began to understand that the challenges and hardships I had faced were not obstacles to be overcome, but rather opportunities for growth and transformation. The darkness that once threatened to consume me now served as a backdrop against which the light of God's love shone even brighter. In embracing my faith, I discovered that my journey from trash to treasure was not just a personal transformation but a testament to the power of God's unwavering love and grace in shaping the course of my life.

I had changed my lifestyle to a certain degree, but was still into things that caused me to add trash in my life. My mother, a powerful Woman of God at the time, was going to house prayers. She used to practically beg me to attend these house prayers with her, I would politely decline every single time.

This one particular time she asked and because I had felt a push to change heavy that day something in me agreed to attend. I began to express to my mom that if anybody there tried to tell me anything about my life, lifestyle, or convert me over I was going off! I meant that.

When I arrived there was this lady going forth in prayer, now the presence of God was not unfamiliar to me after all I'm a PK.(preacher's kid) As I came in, sat down and just listened, something began to happen to me inside it;s as if I felt a part of me tearing apart. All of a sudden she came to me and began to tell me things no one knew, not even my mother.

She began to tell me that it was now or never, and if I didn't get my life right with God now, I would not make it another year! That spoke heavy to me that day, mainly because the change had already begun in my own space and time. That night I surrendered and gave my life to christ.

And I was so thankful that someone was able to reach me. Sister Connie became my safe place, took me under her wings and began to help me walk this walk of life righteously. She is an amazing Woman of God. God chose her to be the one to help me. At that time, she became my closest friend.

She encouraged me; she would always make sure I stayed in connection with my newfound faith, she would not and did not give up on making me see that nothing that happened to me was my fault. She prayed with me, fasted with me, poured into me, and showed me that the people in my life could be trusted again.

With this new love for God, I was in a new light. I said from the heart God, take all this hurt, pain, and darkness! God set me free, and after staying connected to Connie and building a spiritual connection with Him, I was so much lighter, my burdens were lifted.

I let the entire landfill of trash in my life go completely. I started a different journey in life, one that was familiar because my mom was a Woman of strong faith in God. I knew of spirituality and faith in God through her, but I didn't have my own relationship with GOD.

I began to read and study the bible and get an understanding and revelation. I became one with God. I never had an experience, a joy like that ever. Nothing could compare to the love of God that I now have personally.

Life led me to this treasure. I was able to breathe, heal, and forgive. Something that I never did before. Once I took the trash in my life to the landfill of "No more' my eyes saw a whole new world. I was able to love properly and be the woman I was designed to be. I was able to be a good wife, mother, sister, and friend. I was ready to retrieve my treasure, and I have been walking in my happy place, knowing that all life has given me.

I reversed the curse, and my children will never ever have to experience that side of darkness. I took authority over my life, accepted who I am and embraced me. I received the greatest gift I could ever receive, **FREEDOM.** (A true form of treasure)

CHAPTER- 10
EMBRACING REDEMPTION

"FROM CHAINS TO WINGS"

As we reflect on the trash that once burdened our souls like heavy chains, we realize that the key to unlocking our treasure trove of joy and fulfillment lies in the act of forgiveness. It is only through forgiveness that we release the grip of the past on our present, freeing ourselves from the shadows of resentment and anger that once colluded our vision. The solution to forgiving all those who have caused us pain and embracing our own healing lies in the profound understanding that forgiveness is not about condoning the wrongs done to us but about setting ourselves free.

By extending forgiveness to others and,

most importantly, to ourselves,we open our hearts to the transformative power of love, compassion, and grace. In doing so, we pave the way to fully embracing and enjoying the treasures of life- joy, peace, love, and freedom- that have always awaited us just beyond the shadows of our past.

Who I am today is a Woman of strength; when I look back, I thank God for the trials and tragedies; I could not be who I am today without that part of my life. I am healed and whole. I'm a wonderful wife, mother, sister, and friend. I'm grateful for the time it took for me to get here. The old me would be in a sinking dark place. Depressed and blaming my attacks instead of facing them and releasing them. One thing I would tell my old self is You made it! You didn't let what you went through bury you. Look at you, an amazing woman, a Royal priesthood; you are one of a kind, and I love you.

As I stand here at the culmination of my journey From Trash to Treasure, I am enveloped in a profound sense of peace and gratitude that words alone cannot capture. Through the transformative power of forgiveness –both for myself and others– I have unearthed a treasure far more precious than any material wealth could offer. In releasing the weight of past hurts and mistakes, I have discovered a newfound freedom that has allowed me to rise above the ashes of my past and embrace a future filled with hope and possibility.

As I look back on the twists and turns of my path, I am reminded of the countless moments where I faltered and stumbled, where the darkness threatened to engulf me once more. Yet, through the grace of God and the unwavering strength of my faith, I found the courage to confront my fears and confront the shadows that once held me captive. In embracing forgiveness as a beacon of light in the darkest of times, I have unlocked a treasure trove of joy, love, and peace that surpasses all understanding.

CHAPTER- 11
EMBRACING THE INNER LIGHT

In the depths of my own journey, "From Trash to Treasure", I navigated a complicated path of emotions and experiences that ultimately led me to unlock the profound qualities of love, joy, and peace within myself. It was not a simple or linear path but rather a complex journey of self-discovery and growth.

Through moments of vulnerability and introspection, I unearthed buried wounds and fears, allowing me to heal and release the chains that bound me. As I embraced the practice of faith, gratitude, and self-reflection, a subtle transformation began to take root within me.

I realized that love, joy, and peace were not elusive ideas to be chased after by inherent aspects of my being waiting to be embraced.

By cultivating a deep sense of self-awareness and compassion, I found that I could tap into an infinite wellspring of love that radiates outwards, bringing joy and peace into my life and the lives of those around me.

My earnest desire in sharing this intimate part of my journey is to inspire and encourage my readers to embark on their own quest for inner peace and fulfillment, knowing that the keys to unlocking love, joy, and peace lie within their own hearts, waiting to be discovered and celebrated.

CHAPTER- 12
PRESS ON TOWARDS THE MARK

While on this transformative journey, remember that within you lies the power to turn your life around, to shed the weight of past burdens, and to embrace the limitless possibilities that await you. The path to a new level of joy, peace, and fulfillment begins with a willingness to let go of what no longer serves you and to open your heart to new beginnings.

Through the application of the 6 steps outlined in this book, you have the opportunity to declutter your mind, release toxic emotions, and pave the way for a brighter future.

Just as one must clear out the trash to make room for treasures, so too must you let go of negativity and embrace positivity to discover the true gems that life has to offer.

Each step you take brings you closer to a more authentic and empowered version of yourself. Embrace the process, trust in your inner strength, and know that with each decision to move forward, you are creating space for miracles to unfold in your life.

Remember, you are deserving of all the beauty and abundance that life has in store for you. Embrace the journey, have faith in yourself, and allow the transformation to take place.

The treasures of life are waiting for you to claim them – it's time to let go of the trash and welcome the new beginning that awaits.

With courage, determination, and a heart full of hope, you are well on your way to a life filled with purpose, passion, and joy. Believe in yourself, take the leap, and watch as the treasures of life unfold before your eyes. Wishing you strength, peace, and abundance on your journey.

The 6 Steps you can take to maintain a positive and free mindset after achieving this level of emotional healing.

1. **Practice Gratitude:** Cultivate a daily gratitude practice by reflecting on the things you are thankful for in your life. This can help you focus on the positive aspects of your life and maintain a sense of appreciation.

2. **Mindfulness and Meditation:** Engage in mindfulness and Meditation practices to help you stay present in the moment and cultivate inner peace. These practices will help you manage stress, increase self-awareness, and promote emotional well-being.

3. **Surround Yourself with Positivity:** Surround yourself with positive influences, whether it's through the people you spend time with, the media you consume, or the environments you choose to be in. Positive energy can help reinforce your newfound sense of freedom and lightness.

4. **Self-Care:** Prioritize self-care activities that nurture your mind, body, and spirit. This can include activities like exercise, healthy eating, adequate sleep, hobbies you enjoy, spending time in nature, and engaging in activities that bring you joy.

5. **Set Boundaries:** Establish healthy boundaries in your relationships and commitments to protect your emotional well-being. Learning to say no when necessary and setting limits on what you can handle can help you maintain your newfound sense of freedom and peace.

6. **Continuous Learning and Growth:** Engage in continuous learning and personal growth activities that challenge you and help you evolve as a person. This can include reading books, attending workshops, learning new skills, or pursuing hobbies that expand your knowledge and perspective.

By incorporating these steps into your daily life, you can continue to nurture your mind, body, and spirit after finding forgiveness and lightness in your heart. Remember that emotional healing is a journey, and it's important to be patient and kind to yourself as you continue to grow and evolve.

CHAPTER- 13
EMBRACING AUTHENTICITY

"LIVING FULLY IN MY TRUTH"

It took me a while to get here, no it was not an easy journey, it was necessary but definitely not an easy one. Truth be told, all these paths I've taken could have caused me my life multiple times, but with God, incorporating more positivity in my own life and in some odd way the death of my Father. I found my personal treasure. Me, living in my truth unapologetically and free from the trash that weighed me down so many years. Take this journey with me, this is how I was able to embrace change and life free from so much trash in my landfill called life.

Losing my father in February of 2023 was a profound tragedy that shattered my world and forced me to confront the deep-seated pain and unresolved emotions that had accumulated in my life. In the wake of this loss, I found an unexpected wellspring of strength and courage that propelled me towards living authentically and embracing my truth with unwavering determination. It was as if the weight of my grief had unearthed a newfound resolve within me, urging me to confront the accumulated 'trash' in my life and clear the path for the treasures that lay ahead.

As I navigated the process of grieving for my father, I realized that in order to honor his memory and the promise I made to him, I needed to release the burdens of the past that had been weighing me down. It was a journey of introspection and self-discovery, a process of reviewing and reflecting on the experiences and emotions that had shaped me, and letting go of anything that no longer served my growth and well-being. By disposing of the 'trash' in my life, whether it be regret, resentment, or fear. I created space for the treasures of love, forgiveness, and gratitude to flourish.

My promise to my father was not just

a vow of forgiveness and acceptance, but a commitment to living the next phase of my life in alignment with my true self and God's intended path for me. Through this transformative journey of healing and self-discovery, I learned that true strength lies in vulnerability, authenticity, and the willingness to confront the darkest corners of our hearts with courage and compassion. By embracing this phase of my life as a sacred gift and an opportunity for growth, I have embarked on a new chapter filled with hope, resilience, and a deep sense of purpose that guides me towards living fully in the treasures of my life.

CHAPTER- 14
THE STRAIGHT WAY

Embracing authenticity and living fully in your truth is a transformative journey that begins with a deep sense of self-awareness and acceptance. It's about shedding societal expectations and embracing who you truly are at your core.

As you embark on this path, you may find that it requires courage and vulnerability to step into your true self, but the rewards are immeasurable. Living authentically means honoring your values, passions, and beliefs, even if they may differ from those around you.

When you embrace authenticity, you free yourself from the constraints of living a life that is not aligned with your true essence. It allows you to express your thoughts, feelings, and desires openly and unapologetically. By living authentically, you invite genuine connections into your life, as you attract people who appreciate you for who you are, rather than who you pretend to be. This authenticity fosters deep and meaningful relationships built on trust, respect, and mutual understanding.

Living fully in your truth also involves embracing vulnerability and being willing to show up as your authentic self, even in the face of challenges or judgment. It requires a commitment to honesty and integrity in all aspects of your life, as you strive to align your actions with your values and beliefs. By living authentically, you cultivate a sense of inner peace and self-acceptance that radiates outward, inspiring others to do the same.

As you continue to embrace authenticity and live fully in your truth, you may find that your life becomes more purposeful and fulfilling. You begin to make choices that align with your true self, leading to a greater sense of happiness, fulfillment, and inner harmony. By honoring your uniqueness and expressing your true essence, you contribute to a more authentic and compassionate world, where individuality is celebrated and diversity is embraced.

In essence, embracing authenticity and living fully in your truth is a journey of self-discovery, empowerment, and growth. It is a path that invites you to embrace your vulnerabilities, celebrate your strengths, and honor the essence of who you are. By living authentically, you not only enrich your own life but also inspire others to do the same, creating a ripple effect of authenticity and truth in the world around you.

CHAPTER- 15
DIVINE TRANSFORMATION

TRUSTING GOD, FINDING TRUE TREASURE

Losing my father was a profound turning point in my spiritual journey, leading me to a deeper connection with God that has become the cornerstone of my life. In the midst of grief and loss, I found solace and strength in my faith, leaning on God's unwavering love and guidance to navigate the tumultuous emotions and challenges that accompanied my father's passing. It was through this crucible of pain and sorrow that I discovered a profound sense of peace and comfort in surrendering to God's plan, trusting in His wisdom and grace to lead me through the darkness towards the light.

As I delved deeper into my relationship with God, I began to understand that true freedom from the 'trash' of life—whether it be emotional baggage, negative patterns, or self-limiting beliefs—came from surrendering it all to the Divine and allowing His love to cleanse and transform me from within. Through prayer, reflection, and a deepening sense of trust in God's providence, I learned how to identify the toxic elements in my life and release them with faith and courage, knowing that God's grace would guide me towards a path of healing, growth, and renewal.

Trusting in God to be my all in life became not only a source of comfort and strength but also a compass that guided me towards my true treasure—the unshakeable faith and love that transcends all earthly possessions and circumstances. By placing my trust in God as my ultimate source of security, wisdom, and love, I have found a profound sense of peace and fulfillment that surpasses all understanding. Through this journey of faith and surrender, I have learned that my true treasure lies not in material wealth or worldly success, but in the unconditional love and grace of God that sustains me through all trials and triumphs.

Today, as I stand free of the 'trash' that once burdened my heart and mind, I am grateful for the transformative power of loss and faith that has led me to this place of deep spiritual connection and inner peace. With God as my guiding light and true treasure, I move forward with confidence and gratitude, knowing that His love is the ultimate source of strength, wisdom, and joy in my life.

AN EXORT TO MY QUEENS

Women never in a million years would have known that one of my calling would be that of the encourager, being where I am in life now I realize that all those years in the world of darkness I was walking in my call all along, I was just working for the wrong entity. Here's an exhortation for you to read and be encouraged the more on your journey From Trash To Treasure.

In a world that often seeks to define and limit you, remember that you are a force of nature, a beacon of strength, and a source of endless inspiration. Embrace the power that lies within you, for you are capable of achieving greatness beyond measure. Your journey is unique, your story is valuable, and your presence in this world is essential.

In the face of adversity, remember that you possess a resilience that knows no bounds. Your ability to persevere, to overcome obstacles, and to rise above challenges is a testament to your incredible spirit and unwavering determination. Do not be afraid to stand tall, to speak your truth, and to assert your worth. Your voice is powerful, your perspective is invaluable, and your contributions are indispensable.

As you navigate through life's twists and turns, remember to be kind to yourself, to celebrate your victories, and to learn from your setbacks. Surround yourself with a supportive community of like-minded individuals who uplift and empower you. Together, you can create a network of strength and solidarity that will help you weather any storm and conquer any mountain.

Believe in your dreams, no matter how big or bold they may seem. Trust in your abilities, your intuition, and your innate wisdom to guide you towards fulfilling your aspirations. Take risks, challenge the status quo, and dare to be unapologetically yourself in a world that often demands conformity. Your authenticity is your superpower, and your uniqueness is your greatest gift to the world.

Remember that you are enough, just as you are. You do not need to conform to society's narrow standards of beauty, success, or worthiness. Your value lies in your inherent worth as a human being, in your compassion, in your intelligence, and in your capacity to love and be loved. Embrace your flaws, your imperfections, and your vulnerabilities, for they are what make you beautifully human.

As you journey through life, remember that you are never alone. Countless women before you have paved the way, broken barriers, and shattered glass ceilings so that you may walk your path with greater freedom and opportunity. Honor their legacy, learn from their wisdom, and carry their torch forward with pride and determination.

The world is waiting for your light to shine bright. Do not dim your radiance for anyone or anything. Embrace your power, your purpose, and your potential with open arms. Be bold, be fearless, and be unapologetically you.

You have the strength, the courage, and the resilience to create a future that is bright, equitable, and full of possibilities. The world needs your voice, your vision, and your leadership now more than ever. Go forth and conquer, knowing that you are unstoppable, you are extraordinary, and you are enough.

The future is yours to shape, and the possibilities are endless. Embrace them with open arms and a fierce heart. You are a force to be reckoned with, and the world is a better place because of you. Rise, shine, and soar to new heights, for you are truly a wonder to behold."

AN EXORT FOR THE MEN

To the Men that will read my journey, the same applies, I had such an impact in the world. When I allowed myself to be healed from the pain that some men caused in my life and forgive not only them but myself, I saw the true value to what you as a Man bring to all you encounter.

That allowed me to trust again and some of my most dearest friends were men. I was able to be there to listen and give advice which allowed them to become free and open. I truly thank God for the gift of encouragement because it was necessary for the ones in my life. So I exhort encouragement to you as well.

Men, you possess an innate strength, resilience, and capacity for greatness that is truly remarkable. Embrace your unique qualities, honor your values, and strive to be the best version of yourself in all aspects of life. Remember that vulnerability is not a weakness but a sign of courage and authenticity. Allow yourself to feel, to express, and to connect on a deeper level with those around you.

In a world that often expects you to be stoic and unyielding, know that it is okay to seek help, to express your emotions, and to prioritize your mental and emotional well-being. True strength lies in acknowledging your vulnerabilities, seeking support when needed, and fostering healthy relationships built on trust, respect, and open communication.

As you navigate the complexities of life, remember to lead with integrity, compassion, and empathy. Use your voice and your actions to champion equality, justice, and inclusivity for all. Stand up against injustice, discrimination, and violence in all its forms, and strive to be a positive force for change in your community and beyond.

Embrace your role as a mentor, a partner,

a friend, and a leader with humility and grace. Listen actively, speak with kindness, and uplift those around you with words of encouragement and support. Be a role model for the next generation, showing them what it means to be a man of character, integrity, and compassion.

In your pursuit of success and fulfillment, remember to prioritize your physical, mental, and emotional well-being. Take time to rest, recharge, and engage in activities that bring you joy and fulfillment. Cultivate healthy habits, set meaningful goals, and strive for balance in all areas of your life.

Above all, remember that you are enough just as you are. Your worth is not defined by societal expectations, material possessions, or external validation. Your true value lies in your character, your integrity, and the impact you have on the lives of those around you.

Men, the world needs your strength, your compassion, and your leadership now more than ever. Embrace your role as a positive force for change, a champion for equality, and a beacon of hope in a world that is in need of healing and transformation.

Stand tall, stand strong, and stand together with those who share your values and your vision for a better future. You have the power to make a difference, to inspire others, and to leave a lasting legacy of positivity and progress.

Embrace that power, harness it for good, and let your light shine bright for all to see. You are capable, you are worthy, and you are an essential part of creating a more inclusive, compassionate, and equitable world for all. Rise up, embrace your potential, and lead with courage, compassion, and conviction.

The world is counting on you to be the change you wish to see. Go forth with confidence, humility, and a commitment to making a positive impact. You are a force to be reckoned with, and the future is brighter because of you.

INVOKE THE SPIRIT WITHIN

In my journey, the one thing I wish I had done earlier in life was to gain a relationship with God for myself, instead of turning away from Him. I've always known of God, but did not have my own relationship with Him. But as I began my walk with God, I understood that prayer is essential to the betterment of one's life, and now I completely understand that the only way to get to the treasures in life is by allowing God to clean and restore you. One must continue to have an active prayer life. There is a peace like no other when you have tapped into the spiritual realm through prayer. So here is a gift to you **PRAYERS!** To help make it a little bit easier for you to take on this thing called life. Read them daily, apply them to your life, and trust that through faith, it shall work out for your good.

A PRAYER
FOR REDEMPTION

"Heavenly Father,

I come before you with grateful hearts,

Seeking guidance and strength in our journey.

May our readers learn to take the trash in their lives,

Dispose of it properly, and find the hidden treasures

That You have in store for them.

Grant them the courage to forgive themselves,

To release the burdens of the past,

And to embrace the redemption and grace You offer.

May they walk in the light of Your love,

And may Your blessings overflow in their lives.

Guide them on the path to self-discovery,

Help them uncover the beauty within,

And lead them to the abundant life You promise.

In Your mercy and wisdom, transform their struggles

Into stepping stones toward a brighter future.

May this book be a beacon of hope and inspiration,

A reminder of Your unfailing love and compassion.

Bless each reader with Your peace and joy,

And empower them to rise above their challenges,

Embracing the treasure of Your grace.

In Your holy name we pray, Amen"

A PRAYER
FOR CONDEMNATION

"Heavenly Father,

I come before you today seeking your grace and mercy. I confess that at times, the spirit of condemnation weighs heavy on my heart and mind, causing me to doubt my worth and your love for me. Lord, I ask for your forgiveness for any self-condemnation or negative thoughts that have clouded my mind.

I pray that you fill me with your peace and reassurance, reminding me of your unending love and grace. Help me to silence the voice of condemnation and instead hear your voice of truth and compassion. Give me the strength to reject feelings of guilt and shame, knowing that through your Son Jesus Christ, I am forgiven and made new.

May your Holy Spirit guide me in replacing self-condemnation with self-compassion and self-forgiveness. Help me to see myself through your eyes - as a beloved child, worthy of love and redemption. Grant me the courage to let go of past mistakes and embrace the freedom that comes from your unconditional love.

I surrender my fears and insecurities to you, trusting in your promise of redemption and restoration. Thank you, Lord, for your never-ending mercy and grace. In Jesus' name, I pray. Amen."

May this prayer bring you comfort, strength, and a renewed sense of God's love and forgiveness in your life.

A PRAYER TO ROOT OUT BETRAYAL

"Heavenly Father,

I come before you in the name of Jesus, seeking your strength and guidance. I confess any feelings of betrayal in my heart and ask for your help in rooting out the spirit of betrayal that may be influencing my thoughts and actions.

I pray for wisdom and discernment to recognize any seeds of betrayal within me or around me. Help me to forgive those who have betrayed me and to release any bitterness or resentment from my heart.

Fill me with your love, grace, and mercy so that I may extend forgiveness and understanding to others. Protect me from the temptation to betray others and help me to always act with integrity and honesty.

I surrender myself to you, Lord, and ask for your healing touch to cleanse me of any traces of betrayal. Strengthen me to walk in your ways and to show love and kindness to all those around me.

Thank you, Lord, for your faithfulness and for hearing my prayer. I trust in your power to deliver me from the spirit of betrayal and to fill me with your peace and joy. In Jesus' name, I pray, Amen."

Remember, prayer can be a powerful tool for seeking strength and guidance in times of struggle.

A PRAYER TO
ROOT OUT UNFORGIVENESS

"Heavenly Father,

I come before you in the name of Jesus, acknowledging the presence of unforgiveness in my heart. I confess my struggle to let go of past hurts and release the burden of forgiveness that weighs heavy on my soul.

I ask you, Lord, to grant me the strength and grace to forgive those who have wronged me. Help me to see them through your eyes, with compassion and understanding, and to release any bitterness, anger, or resentment that I may be holding onto.

Fill me with your love and peace, Lord, so that I may extend forgiveness freely and unconditionally, just as you have forgiven me. Grant me the wisdom to know when to seek reconciliation and when to let go and move forward in peace.

I surrender my pain and my unforgiveness to you, Lord, and I ask for your healing touch to cleanse me of these negative emotions. Help me to walk in forgiveness, to love my enemies, and to show grace and mercy to all those around me.

Thank you, Lord, for your unfailing love and your power to help me root out unforgiveness from my heart and fill me with your peace and joy. In Jesus' name, I pray, Amen."

Remember that forgiveness is a process, and it's ok to seek God's help and guidance along the way.

A PRAYER TO ROOT OUT THE SPIRIT OF OFFENSE

"Heavenly Father,

I come before you seeking guidance and strength to overcome the spirit of offense that burdens my heart. Help me to release any feelings of anger, resentment, or hurt that may be weighing me down.

Grant me the wisdom to see beyond the actions of others and to understand that their words or deeds are not a reflection of my worth. Help me to cultivate compassion and empathy towards those who have caused me pain.

Fill me with your peace and love so that I may respond to offense with grace and forgiveness. Grant me the clarity to recognize when I am asked about the risk of taking offense and the strength to choose a path of understanding and acceptance instead.

May your light shine upon me and guide me towards healing and wholeness. I surrender my pain and anger to you, knowing that with your help, I can overcome the spirit of offense and live a life filled with love, compassion and understanding.

Thank you for your presence in my life and for the strength you provide me each day.

Amen."

Remember that prayer can be a powerful tool for seeking comfort, guidance, and healing in times of distress.

A PRAYER TO HELP WITH INSECURITIES AND LOW SELF-ESTEEM

"Heavenly Father,

I come before you in humility, seeking your guidance and strength to overcome my insecurities and low self-esteem. You know the depths of my heart and the struggles that weigh heavy on my spirit.

Lord, I confess my feelings of inadequacy and self-doubt. Help me to see myself as you see me - fearfully and wonderfully made in your image. Grant me the courage to embrace my worth and value as your beloved child, deserving of love and respect.

Fill me with your light and truth, Lord, to dispel the darkness of negative self-perception. Help me to replace self-criticism with self-compassion, self-doubt with self-confidence, and insecurity with inner strength.

Teach me to focus on my strengths and to celebrate the unique gifts and talents you have blessed me with. Guide me to walk in the path of self-acceptance and self-love, knowing that I am enough just as I am.

Heal the wounds of the past that have contributed to my insecurities and low self-esteem. Grant me the wisdom to let go of self-limiting beliefs and to embrace a mindset of positivity and empowerment.

I surrender my insecurities and low self-esteem to you, Lord, and I ask for your transformative touch to renew my mind and spirit. Help me to see myself through the lens of your unconditional love and grace.

Thank you, Lord, for your unending love and for the strength you provide in times of weakness. May your presence empower me to rise above my insecurities and walk confidently in the truth of who I am in you.

In Jesus' name, I pray, Amen."

May this prayer bring you comfort, healing, and a renewed sense of self-worth and confidence. Remember that you are valued

and cherished by a loving God who created
you with purpose and intention.

A PRAYER TO
PRAY FOR SUICIDAL THOUGHTS

"Heavenly Father,

In my moments of deepest despair and darkness, I turn to You for comfort and strength. Please help me see the light in the midst of this darkness and guide me to a place of peace and hope.

Grant me the strength to endure my struggles and the courage to seek help when I need it. Help me to remember that I am loved, valued, and never alone, even in my darkest moments.

Fill me with your peace that surpasses all understanding and reminds me of the purpose and value of my life. Give me the wisdom to know that there is always hope and help available to me, even when it feels out of reach.

I surrender my pain, my fears, and my doubts to You, knowing that You are a God of compassion and love. Please surround me with Your healing presence and lift me up when I am feeling overwhelmed.

Help me to find the strength to keep going, one step at a time, knowing that You are with me always. Amen."

Remember, it's important to reach out for professional help and support when dealing with suicidal thoughts. You are not alone, and there are people who care about you and want to help you through this difficult time.

SELF-LOVE POEM

In the mirror, I see a soul so true, With flaws and imperfections, but beauty too.

I embrace myself with kindness and care, For in self-love, I find strength to bear.

I cherish the essence of who I am, Unique and special, a rare kind of gem. With each heartbeat, I choose to believe, In my worth and potential,

I freely receive. I am enough, just as I am, With all my scars and dreams that span.

In self-love's embrace, I find my light, A beacon of love that shines so bright.

May this poem inspire you to love and appreciate yourself just as you are.

Tosha Smith

FROM TRASH TO TREASURE

CONCLUSION

Today, as I bask in the radiant glow of redemption and renewal, I am reminded that the journey from trash to treasure was never about the destination but rather the transformation that occurred along the way.

In letting go of the burdens that weighed me down and embracing forgiveness as a path to healing,

I have uncovered the true essence of my being – a radiant soul, shimmering with the light of divine love and grace. And in this newfound treasure,

I have found not only redemption for my past, but a promise of a future filled with boundless joy and infinite possibilities. A true transformation **From Trash To Treasure.**

"May you always remember that amidst the piles of trash, life may sometimes heap upon you, the power to uncover your true treasure lies within you.

Embrace the journey, trust in your strength, and never underestimate the resilience of your spirit. Your story is still being written, and within its pages, the most precious gems await discovery.

Keep moving forward with unwavering belief in yourself, for your treasure is waiting to be found. You are the author of your destiny; let your inner light guide you toward the abundant treasures that await. Shine on, brave soul, and may your path be filled with hope, courage, and the unwavering belief in your own limitless potential."

As the song goes, It ain't about how fast you get there ain't about what's waiting on the other side It's the Climb! Keep moving, keep climbing, keep the faith. KEEP YOUR FAITH!

With love, A healed vessel

ABOUT THE AUTHOR

Tosha Smith, is an entrepreneur whose diverse ventures and accomplishments showcase her dedication to empowerment, and community impact. As the CEO/ Founder of Women Who Rock Arkansas DBA Women Who Rock Global Tosha has made significant strides in the communities and surrounding areas, providing assistance to women, youth and young adults.

Expanding her entrepreneurial footprint, Tosha also owns Scarlett Rose, an online luxury shoe and accessory boutique that reflects her exceptional taste and understanding of fashion trends.

Tosha's commitment to women's empowerment is embodied in her non-profit organization which fosters a supportive community for women to thrive and succeed. While her advocacy tends further with her established Talk Show "Wisdom Speaks," a platform featured on Dominion Now television and Facebook live, YouTube, TikTok, X, and Instagram. This platform is dedicated to raising awareness about the struggles in ministry, marriage, stay -at-home moms and real life's situations.

Recognized for her contributions and impact to her customers & community, Tosha has been nominated for the West Memphis Elite Award and has received the Elegance of A Woman Award. Her professional credentials include being a Certified Quality Control Auditor, Owner operator of a top rating cleaning company M & T Professional Cleaning Service, a role in which she helps companies with strategy, structure, safety precautions, and professional cleaning.

She's a Business Consultant Business where she offers mentorship, helps those looking to start a business, maintain a business, and organizations ready to set up structure and wanting to attain a 501 (c)(3) tax exempt status.

In addition to her entrepreneurial and advocacy work, Tosha is a successful 3 time Award winning Author and digital content creator, she produces engaging, influential, & business content for her audience to benefit from.

Tosha's versatility extends to her expertise as a self-taught creator, where her skill and passion for creation are evident. Her journey is marked by a relentless pursuit of excellence, a commitment to empowering others, and a passion for creating positive change across various domains.

Made in the USA
Columbia, SC
01 October 2024

42710986R00059